Isaiah Thomas: The Inspiring Story of One of Basketball's Most Prolific Point Guards

An Unauthorized Biography

By: Clayton Geoffreys

Table of Contents

Foreword

Everyone loves an underdog story. They're demonstrations of grit and perseverance, and displays of pure human spirit. Isaiah Thomas' ascent as one of the best scorers in today's game is a testament to hard work. Thomas' ability to create offense for himself, despite being just 5' 9'' in stature, is truly inspirational. His calm demeanor and active leadership on the court makes him one of the best point guards in today's game. Thank you for purchasing *Isaiah Thomas: The Inspiring Story of One of Basketball's Most Prolific Point Guards*. In this unauthorized biography, we will learn Isaiah Thomas' incredible life story and impact on the game of basketball. Hope you enjoy and if you do, please do not forget to leave a review!

Also, check out my website at claytongeoffreys.com to join my exclusive list where I let you know about my latest books. To thank you for your purchase, you can go to my site to download a free copy of *33 Life Lessons: Success Principles, Career Advice & Habits of Successful People*. In the book, you'll learn from some of the greatest thought leaders of different industries on what it takes to become successful and how to live a great life.

Cheers,

Clayton Geoffreys

Visit me at www.claytongeoffreys.com

Introduction

The world loves an underdog. People always cheer for the man who fights against all the odds and those that defy the usual standards. Underdogs are never more beloved than in the world of sports, where guys that defy physical standards always get the adoration of the masses. Basketball is one of the sports that is never short of an underdog.

In the game of basketball and a professional league such as the NBA, physical gifts have always made superstars out of the athletes. You talk about Shaquille O'Neal, who stood over 7 feet tall and weighed over 320 pounds of mass. Then there is LeBron James, who is 260 pounds of muscle but runs like a gazelle on the hard floor. Russell Westbrook may not be the tallest guard on the floor, but he is lightning quick and jumps out of the building. The best superstars have always been some of the most physically gifted athletes in the history of the game.

The NBA has always been like that. It assesses the players' potential first and foremost based on what his physical attributes could accomplish. His height and wingspan are measured. They look at how physically ready his body is for a tough grind in the league. They assess how fast he could run and how high he could leap. After all, basketball has always been one of the sports that rely chiefly on an athlete's physical gifts.

However, there have been defiant basketball superstars that excelled despite what their physical attributes would tell them. Nate Robinson, who stood barely 5'9", became the first ever player to win the Slam Dunk Contest three times. His predecessor, Spud Webb, won it back in 1986 despite standing 5'6". Damon Stoudamire, who stood 5'10", won the Rookie of the Year award back in 1996. Even Earl Boykins and Muggsy Bogues, who are two of the shortest players in league history, were able to make an impact in the NBA despite their meager size.

While these players are not the shortest, guards like Isiah Thomas, Allen Iverson, and Chris Paul were able to forge superstar careers in the NBA. Thomas led the Detroit Pistons to back-to-back titles in the 80's and is considered one of the greatest players of all time despite being one of the shorter point guards of his era. Allen Iverson won the scoring championship four times in his career and is one of the most resilient and best scorers in the history of the league though he was barely 6 foot tall. And today, Chris Paul is arguably the best pure point guard of his generation even though he stands only 6 feet tall.

Those players were able to defy the usual standards of a league that put a lot of premium on height and physical traits. They made up for their lack of size by playing their heart out on the floor and working hard to hone the fundamental skills that make a basketball player. Instead of relying on what their size dictated them to do, they stood up tall in a league full of giants.

In today's NBA game, the ultimate underdog goes by the name of Isaiah Thomas. At 5'9", nobody even expected the tiny point guard to make it to the NBA. He did not have the freakish athleticism of Nate Robinson, nor was he as lighting   quick as Muggsy Bogues or Earl Boykins. He was coming into the draft as a short player with a lot of heart. But even his heart could not save him from falling all the way to the final pick of the 2011 NBA Draft. He was not even supposed to make it to the NBA.

Despite all the odds stacking against him, Isaiah Thomas made the league when the Sacramento Kings were looking for a serviceable point guard back in 2011. Since then, he slowly proved himself to be a capable scorer despite his height. He was so gritty and determined that he averaged 20 points in his third season with the Kings.

Fast forward to his days with the Boston Celtics, Isaiah Thomas defied his height and all the odds to not only become a good NBA player, but one of the best in the league. He has become a two-time All-Star ever since moving to the Boston Celtics after his stints with the Sacramento Kings and Phoenix Suns. He has not only become an All-Star, but was actually second in the entire league in scoring during the 2016-17 season. With all the seven footers and the freakish athletic forwards and guards in the league, nobody expected a 5'9" point guard to average nearly 30 points a night.

The thing about Isaiah Thomas is that he plays for a team and fan base that is not used to seeing underdogs. The Boston Celtics is a franchise built on history and legacy. It is one of the most storied franchises in the entire NBA alongside the Los Angeles Lakers. All of their best players were never underdogs but were some of the best the league could offer as far as size and skills were concerned.

But here comes Thomas, who was never expected to do much damage in the NBA. He was thrust into the limelight as the most capable player on a very young roster that was building on youth and draft picks. But IT earned the adoration of the crowd just by being himself. He exceeded expectations brought about by his lack of size and became an elite player in an era that banked on the supreme size and athleticism of their point guards. He is not as gifted as most of today's point guards are, but Isaiah Thomas has proven that he belongs in the NBA when nobody in the past even believed he would be drafted.

Chapter 1: Early Life and Childhood

Isaiah Thomas was born on February 7, 1989, in Tacoma, Washington. He was named after NBA legend and all-time great point guard Isiah Thomas, who played for the Detroit Pistons. But it was not because his parents were huge Pistons fans. In fact, it was the opposite. Isaiah's father hated the Detroit Pistons, but was forced to name his son after the legendary point guard.

James Thomas, who only stood 5'6", was a huge Los Angeles Lakers fan. He grew up in Inglewood, which was close to the Forum, where the Lakers used to play. James grew up watching Laker games. As such, he was a huge fan of the purple and gold team. It was the 1988 NBA Finals, which the Los Angeles Lakers won.[i] A few months later, the mother of his unborn child, Tina Baldtrip, was pregnant.

James would make a declaration to his best friend that the Los Angeles Lakers would three-peat and win it all again in 1989. He would put his unborn son's name on the line. As history would show, the Detroit Pistons swept the

Lakers in the 1989 Finals. Isiah Thomas ruled over Magic Johnson in that contest. Hence, James would end up naming his son after the Pistons guard.[i]

Tina, however, had other plans. She liked the name, but wanted it to sound more biblical. Instead of spelling it like the Pistons' guard, she would use the biblical spelling instead. Hence, that was how Isaiah Thomas was named. Tina had a religious background as her grandfather was a Pentecostal pastor. James, despite his ill-betting ways, would come to love the name   . Little did he know that his son would one day became a Celtic, a team he also despised back in the 80's.[i]

James (also named Keith) and Tina would not get married, but would have a healthy civil relationship revolving around their son. Isaiah Thomas would bounce around both families from time to time as both parents took turns in nurturing and developing the soon-to-be superstar. James noticed that his son had a big head and nicknamed him "Bighead." Tina, on her part, did not like the nickname. Instead, she would call her son "Zeke," which was the nickname used by Isiah Thomas himself.[ii]

While neither the Thomas nor the Baldtrip households were never tall families, Isaiah Thomas was not expected to be as short as he was. Back when he was in Naches Trail Elementary School, he was one in the middle pack when it came to height. There were boys taller than him, but there were a lot shorter. However, as years went by, he found himself going down and down the line more.

This did not sit well with James Thomas. Standing only 5'6", Thomas was shorter than Tina, who stood 5'7". He wanted his son to grow taller, but the growth spurt he was waiting for did not come. Instead, he would go on to have his son stretched out by machines hidden inside the household's basement.[ii]

Despite his lack of height, Isaiah Thomas was full of determination. When he was with James, the father and son duo would bond by going to local ballparks when Isaiah was a young teenager. He would play with adults much bigger and more experienced than he was. This did not falter the resolve of the younger Thomas one bit. Isaiah would use this experience as his personal drive. He learned how to score and play against bigger and older players.

The remarkable thing about Isaiah Thomas was that he never changed his game from when he was a kid up to the time he was in the NBA. The same moves he developed and learned in fourth grade are essentially the same ones he uses today in the league. It was the same dribble moves, paint finishes, and floaters. He had already developed himself into a highlight reel as early as his sixth grade.

James would say that, at that young age, his son already had a cocky mouth to match his game. He was not only beating them on the hard floor, but was also mopping the gym with them in the trash-talking game. This did not sit well with the older players who would wait outside the gym for the smaller but better young player. James would then make a habit of picking Isaiah up after games as the bigger men his son was beating would try to take their frustrations out on the smaller boy.[ii] Nevertheless, whatever Isaiah Thomas experienced back then only served to make him a better basketball player.

Isaiah Thomas also spent much of his childhood years emulating point guards and their patented moves. He would use his weekends watching NBA games and learning from the greats such as Tony Parker and Steve Nash. He deconstructed Parker's patented floater, which he often used to score inside the paint. Later on, he tried to emulate Nash's floater as well. He would also learn from other greats that attacking the body of the paint defender allowed him to get some leverage when scoring at the basket. At such a young age, he was learning how to take what the defense gave him and used it to his advantage. He would take those skills to build a legendary high school career.[v]

Chapter 2: High School Career

Isaiah Thomas started high school at Curtis Senior High where he became a local legend as far as basketball was concerned. He was wowing crowds with his array of basketball skills despite standing much shorter than his opponents. It was not until his sophomore year in high school when his legend grew bigger and his name became the main attraction.

People began to flock Curtis High's gym every time there was a game involving Isaiah Thomas. The gym became so crowded that basketball teams had to go through the back door just to get to the court. He was entertaining to watch even as a high school player. It did not seem like his height was hindering him from doing what he wanted on the floor. Of course, that was high school, where competition was not at the highest level.

By the time Isaiah Thomas was a junior, he was already the best high school player in his area. Even with a height disadvantage, he was taking bigger defenders to school while also making shots against the taller athletes down in the paint. He would average 32.8 points in his junior year with Curtis. But his most memorable moment that season was during the semifinals game against Franklin High. Isaiah Thomas tried to will his team to victory by scoring 51 big points. He made 16 of the 31 shots he attempted while also managing to hit eight three-pointers in that game. His performance was so memorable that a local reporter had to do an oral history of that performance.[ii] Everyone in Washington still talks about that game today, as Thomas himself would claim. Sadly, Curtis High would lose that game.

After that junior year with Curtis High, Isaiah Thomas was forced to make a life-changing decision. Along with the success that came with him as a basketball star in Washington was the massive ego that bloated out of nowhere. Isaiah Thomas would develop a figurative big head to match his literally big head. He began to shun authority. He could not care any less about his schoolwork. And while the University of Washington was ready to take him in after he graduated, they could not grant him a scholarship because he was academically ineligible.

Then-Washington State Huskies coach Lorenzo Romar urged James Thomas to change his child's course. They asked him to switch to a school where he would be disciplined as far as listening to authority and focusing in studies were concerned. Despite Isaiah and his mother's dissent to the plan, the young boy transferred. He was only 16 years old, but moving cross country to Connecticut was the right decision as far as basketball was concerned. South Kent School was considered a breeding ground for basketball players that wanted to get college scholarships. The competition there was fiercer. Players were bigger and more talented. However, it did not matter for Thomas.[ii]

Raphael Chillious, South Kent's coach, thought that his little player was full of confidence. He would call Isaiah Thomas cocky and brash. Thomas was so cocky that bigger players would even tell the coach that all they wanted to do was to beat the little kid's butt. Thomas never stopped talking trash. However, that came as part of Isaiah Thomas' package. He did not have a lot of size, but he had a loud bark that he backed up with his game. He would average 31.2 points in that season with South Kent.

Chapter 3: College Career

As promised, the University of Washington would take Isaiah Thomas in after he completed his academic eligibility with South Kent. He was coming in as a 5'8" point guard, but was one of the top high school players in the country. *Scout* would rank him as the second-best high school point guard while *Rivals* ranked him as the 14th best player at his position. As a Husky, he would also wear Nate Robinson's Number 2 jersey with the blessing of the three-time dunk champion, of course. Both players looked eerily similar on the floor given that they were both barely 5'9".

While Isaiah Thomas was regularly the smallest guy on the floor during games in Washington State, he always had the biggest heart and strongest will to compete and score points. As a freshman, he immediately made an impact on his team and was putting up big scoring nights every game. His season high that year was when he was able to score 27 points in a win over Morgan State in the final game of 2008.

Isaiah Thomas would help lead Washington into the NCAA Tournament as a fourth-seeded team. The Huskies would go on to dominate Mississippi State in the opening round. Isaiah Thomas would bring his best game in the second series against Purdue. He would score 24 points against the lower seeded team. However, Purdue ended up besting the Huskies by two points as Isaiah Thomas' first season in college ended in the second round of March Madness.

Nobody expected the way Isaiah Thomas dominated the floor as a 5'9" freshman point guard. He would go on to average 15.5 points, three rebounds, 2.6 assists, and 1.1 steals in his first year with Washington. He would also win the Pac-10 Freshman of the Year award. But despite his early impact as a college player, Thomas still had a long way to go before he would be ready for the NBA. If he were at least 6 feet tall, the numbers he was putting up would have turned heads as far as scouting was concerned. However, the skills he had at that point in his life were still inadequate to take him to the big leagues and to make up for his lack of size.

Come his sophomore year, Isaiah Thomas proved that his freshman season was not a fluke. He was even better as a player, a scorer, and a leader. One of the highlight accomplishments that Thomas achieved that season was that he was able to score more points than any other Husky player's first two seasons in college. He had a total of 1,134 points after the end of the season. No other Husky player had more points than Thomas did in only two years of college. That was an impressive feat considering that he only stands 5'9".

Among Thomas' other accomplishments was that he was named Pac-10 Most Outstanding Player of the season after the performance he put up in the tournament championship game. Thomas would score 16 points and grab three rebounds that game. Overall that season, Isaiah Thomas averaged 16.9 points, 3.9 rebounds, 3.2 assists, and 1.1 steals.

Coming into the NCAA Tournament, Washington was only the 11th in a more competitive setting. Nevertheless, the Huskies were able to beat the sixth-seeded Marquette team in the first round. Thomas had 17 of his 19 points in the first half of that win to help his team reach the second series for a consecutive season under his leadership.

In the second round, it would seem as if the Huskies' season were going to end at the hands of the third-seeded New Mexico squad. But the tables quickly turned as Washington appeared as if they were the higher seeded team. They would dismantle New Mexico thanks to a solid all-around effort from the team's best players. Isaiah Thomas would finish that blowout win with 15 points to help the Huskies reach the Sweet 16 of the Tournament for the first time in five seasons. However, the West Virginia Mountaineers would put an end to the Huskies' incredible run. Thomas would hardly have an impact on that loss.

In his third season with the Washington Huskies, Isaiah Thomas would make history by becoming only one of four players to receive Pac-10, AP All-American, and All-District First Team honors in the same season. Along with that, he was once again the tournament's Most Outstanding Player after he drained the game-winning buzzer-beater in the overtime win against Arizona State in the Pac-10 championship game. He had 28 points in the tournament finals. Overall, he would average 16.8 points, 3.5 rebounds, 6.5 assists, and 1.3 steals that season. He led the Huskies in points, assists, and steals all in one season. Thomas was also a finalist for the Bob Cousy award that season.

In March Madness, Isaiah Thomas would lead the seventh-seeded Washington State Huskies against Georgia. In that win in the first round, Thomas finished with 19 points and seven assists. However, the team would face a tough challenge against the second-seeded North Carolina team that made it all the way to the championship game. In that second round matchup, Thomas tried his best to take his team to the Sweet 16 once again, but ultimately failed by only three points in the final scoring tally. He finished the game with 12 points and eight assists. Overall in the NCAA Tournament, he averaged 15.5 points and 7.5 assists.

Shortly after the NCAA Tournament on March 31, Isaiah Thomas announced that he would be forgoing his final season with the Huskies to declare that he would be entering the 2011 NBA Draft. He would end his three seasons with the Huskies as sixth all-time in scoring with

1,721 points, third all-time with 415 assists, and third all-time with 164 three-pointers made. He averaged 16.4 points, 3.5 rebounds, and four assists in his three seasons with the Huskies. He was the model of consistency as his production never dipped, but only improved in the three seasons he spent with Washington.

Chapter 4: NBA Career

Getting Drafted

The 2011 NBA Draft was one not particularly extensive as far as talent was concerned, but was dominated by frontcourt players. The backcourt players, especially the point guards, were still one of the main features of the class, but the talent level, aside from consensus top overall pick Kyrie Irving, was not up to par compared to the past and future classes.

As far as point guards were concerned, the primary focus was on Duke's freshman sensation Kyrie Irving, who was wowing scouts and coaches alike with his wizardry with the ball and with his knack for playing the position well, whether it was scoring or passing. He was also coming in as a complete offensive player that had the right size for the position. There was no doubting that the Cleveland Cavaliers were going to take Irving with the top overall pick.

While frontcourt players were the better choices aside from Irving, guards such as Kemba Walker, Brandon Knight, and Jimmer Fredette were also getting consideration for the lottery picks. There were also sleeper first-round prospects such as Klay Thompson and Kawhi Leonard. But as far as the top 10 picks were concerned, only Irving and Walker were able to become All-Stars. The other four All-Stars of that class were taken after the top 10. But one would wonder how far down Isaiah Thomas was taken.

Measured at a generous 5'10" during pre-draft, Isaiah Thomas was 5'9" coming into the 2011 NBA Draft. He was not even the biggest player for his size given that he was about 186 pounds during the measurements. His size alone was already a red flag for teams that wanted to take a point guard in a league that has increasingly been leaning towards backcourt players.

Almost no team took the time to consider taking Isaiah Thomas in the first round or even in the draft. He was not the eye-opener that Kyrie Irving was nor did he have the skills that Kemba Walker had coming into the draft. He was considered an excellent player that has not even found his niche in the game of basketball itself. Thomas was not the best point guard nor was he the best scorer.

While his size best suited him to play the point guard position, Isaiah Thomas spent most of his college days playing the role of a scoring guard. Scoring was always his mentality. That was what made him a legend in Washington. His priority was to put the ball in the basket. The same was true in college. He was called out there on the floor to make buckets. If Allen Iverson was already an undersized scoring guard at 6 feet, Isaiah Thomas was even smaller.

But like Iverson, Thomas had a lot of heart when it came to putting the ball in the basket. He was always considered a crafty scorer that knew where the defensive holes were and how to get to the basket. He had the quickness and burst of speed to blow by defenders whenever he wanted to get inside the paint. Whatever he lacked in height and size, he made up for in speed, much like his small predecessors did.

Whenever Isaiah Thomas got to the basket, he always seemed like he knew what to do. He had excellent ball fakes that could make defenders look twice as he would get himself to the rim. Despite his size, he has a good vertical leap that measures nearly 40 inches. He knows how to use that to his advantage whenever he goes up for a basket. Though he is not the biggest player, he has learned over time how to use his body to shield the ball away from shot blockers at the rim. If not that, he has mastered the art of putting up floaters and runners to evade shot blockers in the paint. Isaiah Thomas puts a lot of heart into his game especially, when he is determined to put the ball in the hoop.

As far as shooting goes, Isaiah Thomas is a proficient marksman. He has shown improvement from the three-point line whenever he was coming off screens or was spotting up. In fact, he is considered one of the best three-point shooters in Washington Huskies history after all the shots he has drained from that distance. And whenever he wanted to come up big in the clutch, his shooting was always one of the best assets to look at.

Given that he was slated to become a full-time point guard if he was ever going to get to the NBA, Isaiah Thomas also showed significant improvement as a playmaker. He was a scoring guard for most of his first two years in college. His priority was always to score the ball. But in his junior year with the Huskies, Thomas was able to show that he had what it took to become a playmaker. He increased his assists numbers significantly and was only getting better as the season went on. Best of all, he did not have to sacrifice his scoring output though he was passing the ball more than he ever did.

Defensively, Isaiah Thomas was never a slacker. He did not have the size to cover players put played position defense well. Thomas had the lateral quickness to keep up with his man and was very hard to push off given his low center of gravity. He showed great anticipation at knowing where his opponents would go considering that he could also quickly change directions.

While there are a lot of aspects that stand out when looking at Isaiah Thomas, especially for teams looking to generate offense from the point guard spot, size is again a factor when it comes to the best basketball league in the world. The NBA level is a much different story than college. Players are a lot bigger, faster, stronger, and more athletic than what Thomas was accustomed to. His lack of size would negate every positive thing he could bring to the floor.

As far as scoring is concerned, Thomas always had the tools to get to the basket and finish strong among the tall players in the paint. However, the problem was that none of the players in college are as quick as the ones in the NBA. Players in the league would be fast enough to keep with Thomas out on the perimeter. He was not as blazing fast as Allen Iverson was, but had enough speed. But it would not suffice in the NBA. Aside from that, if ever indeed he would be able to get to the rim, NBA defenders are bigger, stronger, and better at guarding the paint than the competition that Thomas faced as a Husky. No matter how big of a heart and fight he had in himself, he would be deemed too small to be able to compete against elite level NBA players.

When it came to shooting, Isaiah Thomas might have improved drastically as a spot-up and catch-and-shoot player, but was still mediocre at best when it came to shooting off the dribble.   It was not that he lacked the proper mechanics. Again, size plays a significant factor.

With his lack of size, Thomas needed a lot of separation to get his shot off the dribble. He also had the tendency to lean forward and put a lot of power in his jump to get off a quality shot. When he does that, it takes a lot of room for him to see the basket off the dribble. That was a big problem that Thomas had to try to solve whenever his ability to get to the basket was taken away.

While he has shown improvements as a playmaker, Isaiah Thomas still lacked the tools and IQ necessary to become a full-time point guard in the NBA. He struggled a lot with turnovers back in college because of his tendency to make flashy but bad passes and because he also over-dribbles in several plays. He did not always make the right plays and was still raw as far as playmaking skills went.

Defensively, nobody could discount the heart and expertise he had in that part of the game. However, the NBA is a different story. Players are stronger, faster, and bigger. They could blow by the smaller Thomas out on the perimeter because of the latter's lack of striding length. They could also outmuscle him everywhere on the floor. They could even shoot over the outstretched arms of

Thomas, who only has a wingspan of 6'1". He was going to be a defensive liability in the NBA and was not going to be able to stop anybody from scoring or denying a player from getting the ball.

With all those things considered, Thomas was not a rare player as far as skills were concerned. Other players had the same skillset that he had. Other score-first guards were bigger than he was. Size was always a factor in the NBA. Sadly, Thomas did not have any of that. Teams knew that. They were not going to take a 5'9" scoring guard early on. He had too many red flags for his lack of size alone. He was going to be a liability on the defensive end while he struggles to adjust his offense at the NBA level. But nevertheless, what Thomas had was the heart and competitive fire burning in him. That must have accounted for something as 59 players were called in the 2011 NBA Draft before the Sacramento Kings would take him with the 60th pick. Yes, he was selected 60th—dead last in the 2011 NBA Draft.

The Rookie and Early Seasons, Proving Himself

The Sacramento Kings took their chances with Isaiah Thomas. They were one of the worst franchises in the league at that point but had solid talent to build on. They had a rising sophomore player DeMarcus Cousins, who would soon become the best center in the league. They also had former Rookie of the Year Tyreke Evans trying his best to get to the next level. Other than those two, the Kings relied mostly on scorer Marcus Thornton and veteran small forward John Salmons. They would even acquire college hotshot Jimmer Fredette in a draft day trade.

But what the Kings lacked was a point guard. Evans needed the ball in his hands, but was not the typical playmaker. Thornton and Fredette were both guards that loved to shoot the ball first before passing it. The lack of a point guard was what troubled the roster early on. Nobody fed the ball to Cousins. Nobody could move the rock and make plays. Nobody could disrupt defensive sets to give teammates open looks. This was when Isaiah Thomas came in.

Isaiah Thomas would make his season debut on December 26 when the league had just resumed after a lockout delayed the proceedings. In his first ever game as a professional, he played off the bench for 5 points in only 13 minutes of action. It was in a win against the Los Angeles Lakers. However, over the next four games, he would play sparingly as a backup point guard for the Kings.

It was on January 3, 2012, when Isaiah Thomas showed glimpses of the future All-Star. He would go for a then career high of 15 points together with five rebounds in only 16 minutes of action in a loss to the Memphis Grizzlies. After that game, he deserved the then season-high 28 minutes he played in a loss to the Denver Nuggets. He would only score 4 points that night.

After several more games of barely playing any minutes for the Kings, Isaiah Thomas would break out in a win against the Toronto Raptors on January 11. Playing a little less than 24 minutes that night, he would go for 20 points and six assists. He shot 6 out of 12 from the floor and 3 out of 6 from the three-point line in that new career game for him. Following that performance, he would have 13 points against the Houston Rockets two days later in a loss.

From January 23 until the end of the month, Isaiah Thomas would string together four consecutive games of scoring in double digits. He started by going for 11 points and a then-career best of 8 assists against the Portland Trailblazers. After that, he went for 16 markers and six dimes versus the Nuggets before combining for 24 points in the next two games, which were against the Utah Jazz and the Golden State Warriors. Though the Kings lost all four of those games, there was no questioning that Isaiah Thomas was getting more productive.

The Kings would remedy those four losses by winning the next three games. In the final game of that three-game stretch, Thomas went for 17 points in 26 minutes of play. He shot 6 out of 11 and 3 out of 6 from the three-point line in that win over the New Orleans Hornets on February 6. With performances like those, it was only a matter of time until Thomas would get the recognition he needed and deserved.

On February 17, Isaiah Thomas would finally get his first start as an NBA player. Head coach Keith Smart would bench Jimmer Fredette in place of Thomas, who was drafted 50 spots below the shooter, and Thomas did not disappoint. He went for 13 points on 4 out of 6 shooting from the field in that loss to the Detroit Pistons.

Two days after his first career start, Isaiah Thomas would have another career game. In 43 minutes of play against Kyrie Irving, the 60th pick of the 2011 NBA Draft would thoroughly outplay the top overall pick. He nearly had a triple-double after registering 23 points, eight rebounds, and 11 assists. Thomas shot 8 out of 16 from the floor and 3 out of 7 from the three-point area in a game that narrowed the gap between him and Kyrie Irving.

On February 19, Isaiah Thomas would top his career high by going for 24 points on 7 out of 14 shooting from the field and 5 out of 8 shooting from the three-point area in a loss to the Miami Heat. He would then finish the next four games scoring in double digits to go for a then record of eight consecutive outings of putting up at least 10 points. With such a momentous month of February for him, Isaiah

Thomas became the first ever player to be named Rookie of the Month as the last pick of the draft. He averaged 12.2 points and 4.4 assists that month. He was even better during the month of March after posting 13.6 points and 4.9 assists. Once again, he was the Western Conference Rookie of the Month.

Isaiah Thomas' second career double-double game in a win over the Boston Celtics on March 16. He registered 13 points and ten assists in that outing against his future team. He then had 18 points in the next two games, which were wins against the Minnesota Timberwolves and the Memphis Grizzlies. At that point, he was looking like he was the biggest steal of the draft while players drafted 50 or more spots before him were still struggling.

On March 28, Isaiah Thomas would top his best performance yet again. In that loss to the San Antonio Spurs, IT would go for 28 points on a solid 11 out of 19 shooting clip. He also added ten assists for his third career double-double. He then went on to score in double digits in the next five games. This included his 25-point performance in a loss to the Phoenix Suns on April 3. Then, in the course of his final 11 games, Thomas would score in double digits in all but two of them. Those included two 21-point performances against the OKC Thunder and the San Antonio Spurs. Both were losses.

At the end of the season, Isaiah Thomas was indeed the biggest yet physically smallest steal of the 2011 NBA Draft. He averaged 11.5 points and 4.1 assists in his rookie season. He shot 44.8% from the floor and 38% from the three-point line. Those are terrific numbers for a player his size. Thomas would also be named to the All-Rookie Second Team and finished within the top 10 in the Rookie of the Year voting.

Though the Sacramento Kings were one of the fodder teams during Thomas' rookie season, there was no denying how big of an impact he had in such a small package. Thomas was overlooked coming into the draft particularly because of his size. While size was not always a factor in point guards, his playing style was a red flag. Earl Boykins and Muggsy Bogues were great playmakers in their rights while Nate Robinson had freakish athleticism. Meanwhile,

Thomas was a scoring guard in the size of a miniature point guard.

But Thomas never changed his approach to the game. He never changed his style and his competitive fire.[iii] Even his coaches knew what a gem they had in Isaiah Thomas. Pete Carril, an assistant during Thomas' rookie season, was so impressed with how quick and how good a shooter the 5'9" guard was. He gave a lot of confidence in the little guy by telling him never to get tired and never to lose confidence in putting up shots.[ii] That was Thomas' identity after all. He was a scorer.

Throughout the season, Thomas played with a huge chip on his small shoulders. In the draft, he was passed on 59 total times before a struggling Sacramento Kings decided to try their hand on him. No team wanted him because of his size. The NBA average height is about 6'7". Thomas is nine inches short of that, but size never impeded him from giving his all. In fact, his lack of height was what gave him the fight and the heart he needed to give his all night in and night out.

But Isaiah Thomas was without phases of frustrations when he was a rookie. He had to endure playing behind the struggling Jimmer Fredette at the point guard position for most of the early season. And when he did indeed get the starting spot he was so deserving of, the Kings would put the ball more in the hands of Tyreke Evans. Moreover, Sacramento was not a team that was built to win anytime soon.

Thomas was always a winner. He won championships in high school, and the Huskies were always a part of March Madness in his three years with Washington. But the Kings were different. It was not an environment for winners. Nevertheless, Keith Smart told his rookie never to get caught up with what is happening in the present. Instead, he would ask Thomas to focus on the future and his long-term plans.[ii] Those were words he kept to heart as the miniature player would one day rise to become an elite one.

Having proven himself as a player belonging to the NBA, Isaiah Thomas would come into his second season as an integral part of a Sacramento Kings team looking to build on the young pieces such as Cousins, Evans, and Thomas himself. But after having traded the disappointing Jimmer Fredette over the offseason, the Kings would acquire another point guard by the name of Aaron Brooks, who would share minutes with Thomas at the playmaker position.

As the 2012-13 season started, Isaiah Thomas reprised his role as the team's starting point guard. He would open the season with 10 points in a loss to the Chicago Bulls on opening day. He would bounce back two days later by going for 20 points in a loss to the Minnesota Timberwolves. Thomas would score in double digits in all but one of his first seven games of the season, showing the same kind of consistency he had during his rookie season.

Unfortunately for Isaiah Thomas, he would momentarily lose his starting position and the majority of the minutes he used to play to the more experienced and slightly bigger Aaron Brooks, who was deemed a better playmaker and passer than the score-first guard from Washington. Thomas would play the role of the spark off the bench while Brooks was dominating the minutes at the point guard position.

While Isaiah Thomas' minutes off the bench were inconsistent, he did have great outputs in games where he would play the amount of time deserving of a player of his caliber. On December 7 in 29 minutes of play, he would go for 17 points, five rebounds, and four assists while shooting 5 out of 10 from the floor. All five of his misses came from the three-point line.

Then, after several consecutive games of seeing inconsistent minutes off the bench, Thomas would show that he was the model of efficiency in a loss to the Oklahoma City Thunder on December 14. In only 16 minutes of play, Isaiah Thomas would go on to score 26 points on a remarkable 10 out of 13 shooting clip. He made 4 of his seven three-pointers that game. Two days later, he would march over to the free throw line 15 times and would hit 13 of those freebies to score 20 points in a blowout loss to the Denver Nuggets.

After proving himself as the best player off the bench for Sacramento, Isaiah Thomas would regain the starting point guard position on December 28 in a win over the New York Knicks. He would score 11 points in that game. Two days later in what would be the Kings' final game of the year 2012, Thomas would go on to score a new season high of 27 points after making 10 of his 15 shots. He also added four rebounds and five assists in that huge win over the Boston Celtics.

It would not take too long for Isaiah Thomas to top his career high and score over 30 points for the first time in his career. On January 12, 2013, Thomas would play out of his mind as the only bright spot in a blowout loss to the overpowering Miami Heat squad. Thomas made 13 of his 22 shots and 6 of his eight three-pointers to score 34 big points. But despite that performance, Thomas saw a bit of slump during the month of January after failing to hit the double-digit mark in 8 of his 17 games during that month.

Isaiah Thomas would remedy a bad January by going off during February. He would start the month scoring 24 points in a loss to the Philadelphia 76ers. A little over a week later, he would go on to score 25 points in a win against the Utah Jazz. He made 10 of his 16 shots from the field in that game. Following that performance, he would go for 23 points against the Houston Rockets just a night later. He made all 13 of his free-throw attempts in that game.

Shortly after the All-Star break, Isaiah Thomas would go for 22 points against the heavy San Antonio Spurs defense. Then, on February 22, he would explode for his second career 30-point game. Thomas would make 9 of his 18 field goals and 4 of his six three-pointers to score 30 points in a loss to the Atlanta Hawks. He also added six rebounds and nine assists in that game. Isaiah Thomas finished the month of February scoring in double digits in all but two of the 12 games he played that month.

As the latter part of the season progressed, Isaiah Thomas looked more and more like the future All-Star he was destined to become. On March 5, he would go for 23 points and eight assists in a loss to the Denver Nuggets before going off for 27 points, five rebounds, six assists, and a career best five steals in a win against the Phoenix Suns three days later. Then, in what would become a 42-point blowout win against the Chicago Bulls, he would contribute 22 points in only 28 minutes of play. He followed that performance up with 26 points in a loss to the Lakers on March 17.

On March 21, Isaiah Thomas would put together a then career best of 10 consecutive games of scoring in double digits. He would average an impressive 19.7 points and 5.2 assists during that stretch. He also shot 46% from the floor and nearly 40% from the three-point line during that run. Isaiah Thomas topped the 20-point mark five times during those ten games. Those five games included his third career 30-point game. He had 31 points in a win against the Golden State Warriors on March 27 after making 10 of his 18 field goals. Seven of those field goals came from the three-point line.

At the end of the season, Isaiah Thomas averaged 13.9 points and four assists. While his numbers did not seem impressive at first look, one would factor in how Keith Smart benched him during the early parts of the season in favor of Aaron Brooks. But when Smart decided to start Thomas once again and put the ball in his hands more often while also putting Tyreke Evans off the ball, Thomas boomed and flourished. In the 28 games following the All-

Star break and following the change in the coaching approach, Isaiah Thomas averaged 17.3 points and 5.4 assists. He shot 45% from the floor and over 41% from the three-point line during that stretch. Isaiah Thomas would bring this confidence over to the next season as the Sacramento Kings, who failed to reach the playoffs once again, ended the season early.

The Rise of Isaiah Thomas, Final Year in Sacramento

While Isaiah Thomas had already flourished under Keith Smart during the latter part of his second season with the Sacramento Kings, the franchise had to make certain personnel changes once again. Clashes between franchise player DeMarcus Cousins, authority figures, and coaches had the organization shuffling their staff. They would hire new head coach Mike Malone to try to bring stability to a team that had not become relevant in the league since the early 2000's.

At first, Mike Malone did not believe in what Isaiah Thomas brought to the floor as far as playmaking was concerned. He knew how great a scorer IT was, but decided to relegate him as the first option off the bench in favor of the much bigger and more solid playmaker Greivis Vasquez. But despite playing off the bench, Thomas' minutes and performances were all consistent.

Isaiah Thomas started the season scoring 16 points in 29 minutes off the bench for Sacramento in a win against the Denver Nuggets on October 30. He followed that up with 29 points on an efficient 9 out of 13 shooting clip against the Los Angeles Clippers two nights later. Then, in a loss to the Atlanta Hawks on November 5, Thomas finished with 26 points on a perfect 9 out of 9 shooting from the free throw line. Showing consistency off the bench, Tomas averaged 18.7 points and 4.7 assists in 28 minutes of play during his first 12 games of the season. He scored in double digits in all of those first 12 games. Numbers like those would certainly make Malone think otherwise in deciding to bench him.

On December 7 in a win against the Utah Jazz, Isaiah Thomas was the catalyst off the bench after going for 26 points, eight assists, and four steals. He shot 8 out of 14 from the field in that game. After that performance, Isaiah Thomas finally convinced his new head coach that he deserved to start games. Two nights later, he regained the starting spot and did not disappoint Mike Malone. He would go for his first double-double of the season after registering 24 points and 12 assists in a win over the Dallas Mavericks.

Isaiah Thomas followed that performance up by going for at least 20 points in his next two games. He had 20 markers and seven dimes in a loss to the Jazz on December 11 before going for 29 points on 11 out of 20 shooting from the field in another loss to the Phoenix Suns. But Thomas did not stop there. He would consistently figure himself scoring over 20 points in the first ten games since regaining the starting spot. He would average 21 points, 3.6 rebounds, and 7.5 assists during that 10-game run. Thomas also shot over 47% from the floor and a remarkably impressive 42% from the three-point line since getting the starting spot nod again. He had three double-doubles during that 10-game stretch.

Known primarily as a scorer, Isaiah Thomas had also shown immense growth as a passer and playmaker in his third year in the league. While never sacrificing his scoring output, he would go for good assist nights as a legitimate starting point guard for the Sacramento Kings. He would consistently figure himself above six assists per game. Early in January 2014, there was even a five-game stretch wherein he averaged eight assists per game while also putting up 18 points per night.

But while he had grown considerably as a passer, Isaiah Thomas' game was always predicated on his big heart whenever he wanted to score the basketball. Thomas would have a new career night on January 19. He would make 11 of his 18 field goal attempts, 4 of his eight three-pointers, and 12 of his 13 free throw shots to score a new career best of 38 points in a loss to the Thunder. He followed that up two nights later, recording 20 points and 11 assists for another double-double that season.

Five days after he scored 38 points, Isaiah Thomas did it again. On January 24, Thomas scored 13 of his 31 attempts from the field and made all 10 of his free throws to record and tie his 38-point career best. He also added six assists to his name in that loss to the Indiana Pacers. In the four games he played between those two 38-point outputs, Thomas averaged 29 points and 7.3 assists.

Isaiah Thomas also quietly became one of the more consistent players in the league at that time. From January 15 until March 23, Isaiah Thomas consistently figured himself scoring in double digits. He had remarkable outputs during that stretch while scoring over 20 points in 24 of those outings. He also had his first career triple-double on March 18 after going for 24 points, 11 rebounds, and ten assists in a win over the Washington Wizards. At 5'9", Isaiah Thomas became the shortest player in league history to record a triple-double. That speaks so much to his heart and tenacity for the game of basketball.

Thomas averaged 22.5 points and 6.5 assists during that run, which was cut short because of an injury that had him sitting out ten straight games. Thomas would return to play the final two games of the season, but performed poorly in both outings as the Sacramento Kings were set to miss the playoffs again because of a bad win-loss record.

In his third season with the league, Isaiah Thomas averaged 20.3 points and 6.3 assists. He shot over 45% from the floor and about 35% from the three-point line. Isaiah Thomas also became one of five players under 6 feet tall to average over 20 points per game and over six assists per game in a single season. There was no questioning that Thomas was indeed on the rise at that point of his career.

The Move to Phoenix, the Three Point Guard Lineup

Isaiah Thomas had already more than proven himself as a player that belonged in the NBA. The former last pick of the 2011 NBA Draft had coaches wondering why they never drafted him in the first round or even during the lottery. He was a legitimate top 10 pick if anyone were to rewrite the 2011 NBA Draft all over again. More importantly, he was still young and getting better with experience and hard work. Isaiah Thomas was a bonafide star in the making.

However, the Sacramento Kings had other plans. Isaiah Thomas was on the end of his rookie contract and was a free agent by the end of the 2013-14 regular season. Their best centerpiece was still the big man DeMarcus Cousins, who has grown to become the best center in the league. They also had a capable wing scorer by the name of Rudy Gay, who was acquired early in the past season. They wanted a point guard that thrived in passing the ball first to the team's best scorers instead of one looking to score the ball first. Sadly, Isaiah Thomas was not the playmaker they had in mind.

The Kings never intended to keep Isaiah Thomas for too long. He was regarded as too small for a franchise that wanted to contend for a playoff spot. Sacramento thought he did not play enough defense, that he was not passing the ball well enough, and that he was shooting more than he was asked to. As Thomas himself would say, the Kings were trying to run him out of town the very first chance they got.[iv]

It was just like Draft Day again. Nobody wanted Thomas. Everybody knew what he brought to the table. He was a fearless scorer that attacked the basket fiercely whenever he got the chance to do so. He was a good shooter that was not afraid of big moments. However, his size disadvantage was too much of a red flag for the Kings and several other teams. A 5'9" point guard simply could not keep up with the likes of Stephen Curry, Russell Westbrook, and Kyrie Irving, among others. With that, the Kings would undervalue Isaiah Thomas to someone worth around $5 million a year. Thomas believed he was worth more.

Showing that they had no intention of giving Thomas a bigger contract, the Sacramento Kings would go on to sign Darren Collison during the free agency period, believing he was the better passer compared to Isaiah Thomas. Collison was valued at around $5 million a year. This left Isaiah Thomas a man without a team. Luckily, the Phoenix Suns, who were looking to go back to the run-and-gun offense they were so successful at, were willing to take the 5'9" point guard.

The Phoenix Suns would orchestrate a sign-and-trade deal that brought Isaiah Thomas over to Arizona in exchange for a second round draft pick that amounted to nothing. In essence, the Kings traded away a valued asset for garbage because they never truly saw Isaiah Thomas' value in the first place. The Suns would sign Thomas to a salary worth around $7 million a year.

It was going to be an all new and entirely different culture in Phoenix. The Suns already had two great point guards on the roster. They were both starting Eric Bledsoe and Goran Dragic in the backcourt spots. Neither Bledsoe nor Dragic was less good options than Thomas was at that point of the 5'9" point guard's career. Isaiah Thomas still was not good enough to take away a starting spot from either of those two playmakers. He would play a bench role in Phoenix in his short stint with the Suns.

Realizing they had three good point guards, the Suns would decide to play an even faster pace of basketball much like the 90's when the team had Jason Kidd, Steve Nash, and Kevin Johnson. This meant that they would have to play all three point guards at the same time to the detriment of giving up a lot of size. However, the Suns thought that they had enough speed and quickness to run any team down to the ground with their troika of point guards.

The experiment initially worked. The Suns were able to play well with having to shuffle minutes between three outstanding guards. Thomas himself did not mind playing off the bench. He scored 23 points on 9 out of 11 shooting from the field and 5 out of 7 shooting from the three-point area in his first game as a Sun. He played only 20 minutes in that game while Phoenix would win that one against the Los Angeles Lakers. Two nights later on October 31, he would go on to score 23 points again. In 29 minutes of play, he made 10 of his 17 shots. And as the Suns ran to a 3-1 start, Thomas had 22 points and nine assists in another win against the Lakers on November 5.

However, inconsistency in minutes slowly got to Isaiah Thomas during the first 15 games of the season. He would go on to average 15.5 points and 4.1 assists during that stretch but was barely playing 24 minutes per game. There were nights when he was barely called on to put up heavy minutes or to make an impact on the match. The Suns were 8-7 at that point of the season. Thomas, however, would miss eight consecutive games late in November because of an ankle injury.

Isaiah Thomas would make his comeback on December 12 against the Detroit Pistons. However, he was still obviously hobbled after scoring only 16 points in his first two games since coming back. He would, however, break out by going for 20 points on December 15 in a loss to the Milwaukee Bucks. He then had 23 and 22 points respectively in wins against the Charlotte Hornets and the New York Knicks the next two games. Thomas was quickly getting back to form while the Suns mounted a six-game winning streak. Thomas averaged 16.5 points and 4.2 assists during that stretch.

Things began to look bright again for the Phoenix Suns as the New Year came. They were winning more than they were losing while Isaiah Thomas proved to be the most reliable bench player the league had to offer. He consistently scored in double digits and rarely finished with less than 10 points. In the middle of January, there was even a four-game stretch where he scored 20 or more points in each of those games. He averaged 24.5 points in 30 minutes in those four games.

But, then again, the problem was that the relationship between the Phoenix Suns and Isaiah Thomas was not mutual. Isaiah Thomas wanted to be a starter, but the Suns were also handling things with a disgruntled Goran Dragic. While Phoenix saw success with their three-point guard lineup, it was obviously a relationship that would not last for a long term period. This prompted a trade early in February. As a Sun, Isaiah Thomas averaged 15.2 points and 3.7 assists in 46 games. He started only one game for Phoenix.

The Trade to the Celtics, Rising with Boston

The Boston Celtics were a frontrunner for Isaiah Thomas. General Manager Danny Ainge had long wanted Thomas to be a Celtic ever since he was available during the free agency period. At that point, Ainge had seen a reason as to why the Suns would part with the pint-sized point guard. They would send Marcus Thornton, one of Thomas' former teammates in Sacramento, to the Phoenix Suns in exchange for Isaiah. Technically, the Suns gave Thomas up for a low price, much like how the Kings did. Phoenix also ended up trading away Dragic to the Miami Heat to break up their trio of point guards.

After the trade, the very first person to call Isaiah Thomas was none other than the legendary Isiah Thomas himself. Named after the Pistons legend, Isaiah was happy to hear from a Hall-of-Famer. Isiah told the younger Thomas that he was glad that the small point guard found himself with a real organization that focused on winning and developing their players.[ii] The Celtics have been one of the more storied franchises in the league and have earned the respect of players and coaches alike for being a respectable and professional organization. Boston was where Isaiah Thomas was going to get his fresh start. He would blossom as a Celtic.

At that point of the Boston Celtics' year, they were trying to move away from the Rajon Rondo era that ended when the All-Star point guard was traded earlier in the season. They were looking to rebuild on a very young core of talented players. The Celtics were the most inexperienced team in the league that season. Nobody was over the age of 30 years old. They had a great young core of players that brought the right attitude to the game. It was an organization and a group that would welcome Isaiah Thomas with open arms.

While the Boston Celtics were still trying to adjust Isaiah Thomas into the lineup and system, Head Coach Brad Stevens would choose to start the rookie Marcus Smart, who was drafted sixth overall during the 2014 NBA Draft, instead of the 5'9" point guard, particularly because of his ability to play defense. Nevertheless, Thomas got the minutes he needed and wanted off the bench while he was still trying to adjust to a new system.

Isaiah Thomas would make his Celtics debut on February 22 against no less than the franchise's rivals themselves. In that loss to the Lakers, Thomas had 21 points off the bench in only 25 minutes of play. He shot 6 out of 13 from the floor in that contest. In his return game against the Phoenix Suns just a day later, he would go on to score 21 points and dish out seven assists in 27 minutes off the bench against the team that traded him away just a few days ago. And on February 27, Isaiah Thomas had a new season high of 28 points in a win against the Charlotte Hornets. Thomas averaged 21.8 points and 5.8 assists in his first five games with the Boston Celtics.

The next five games he played for Boston were equally productive. The only time he scored less than 20 points was when he finished with only 11 points in a loss to the Cleveland Cavaliers on March 3. The next four games he played were scored above 20 points. He finished those five games with 21 points and five assists. Overall, he averaged 21.4 points and 5.4 assists in his first ten games with Boston.

Thomas would, unfortunately, miss eight consecutive games because of a bruised lower back. He would make his return on March 25 with only 4 points in a loss to the Miami Heat. But he bounced back by scoring 18 and 19 points respectively against the New York Knicks and LA Clippers the next two games. Though he was getting the minutes and plays he wanted, Thomas would slow down a bit at that point of the season.

On April 8, Isaiah Thomas would score over 30 points for the first time that season. It was also his new season high.

He finished a win against the Detroit Pistons scoring 34 points on 10 out of 17 shooting from the floor, 4 out of 8 shooting from the three-point area, and 10 out of 11 shooting from the free throw line. He did that all while playing less than 30 minutes off the bench.

At the end of the regular season, Isaiah Thomas averaged 19 points and 5.4 rebounds off the bench in the 21 games he played for the Boston Celtics. He totaled 16.4 points and 4.2 assists including the earlier games he played as a Sun. He finished second in voting for the Sixth Man of the Year award but was just as the winner, Lou Williams.

While he was playing bench duties for the Celtics much like he did in Phoenix, there was a noticeable change of role and trust as far as coaching was concerned. Brad Stevens believed in what Isaiah Thomas could do and he thrust him into the role of the team's best scorer and penetrator. The Celtics, who made the playoffs with a 40-42 record, loved what they had in the pint-sized playmaker.

There was a mutual understanding between Isaiah Thomas and the Boston Celtics. It was an understanding that he did not have with the Sacramento Kings, who wanted a player that would feed Cousins and Gay, among others. They wanted a playmaker that passed the ball more than he shot it. They had no room for a scoring point guard like Isaiah Thomas.

The same was true for the Phoenix Suns. Although they loved the speed, quickness, and aggressiveness that Thomas brought to the floor, they relied on two other point guards to give them those qualities. Bledsoe and Dragic were as good as scorers as Isaiah Thomas was at that point of their respective careers. Needless to say, Thomas was the third option in a troika of point guards in Phoenix. Then Boston happened.

The Celtics needed an aggressive player that loved more than anything to shoot the ball and to find gaps in the defense. That was what Isaiah Thomas brought. They did not care how small he was or how he looked to score more than to pass. What they cared about was his aggressiveness. Brad Stevens told him to attack and be aggressive. That was how the other players would feed off of him.

Probably the most memorable part of Thomas' regular season as a Celtic was how he felt he was needed and how he felt that he belonged. It was March 9 against the Miami Heat when he fell hard on his back. The pain was so unbearable that he felt like he did not want to get up. Doctors would even say after the game that it was one of the worst cases of back bruises they have ever seen.[v]

But he heard a voice from a player he had not even been teammates with for a month. "Get up IT, we need you," said forward Jae Crowder.[v] That was how Isaiah Thomas felt he belonged in the Boston Celtics franchise. He always knew he was a star in the making and always believed in what he could do as a player. All he needed was a team that gave him the same confidence. That was what the Boston Celtics did. As the legendary Isiah Thomas would say, the Celtics are a legitimate organization.

The players on the roster were just as confident in Isaiah Thomas' abilities as the Celtics front office. Thomas did not want to get up from that fall. He felt the pain so hard that he thought his night was over. But Jae Crowder's words lit a fuse in him. He got up, drained a free throw and then made a three-pointer. He ended the game with 25 points and a victory for his team. All Isaiah Thomas needed was to feel like he belonged and that he was wanted. He got that with the Boston Celtics even though he had not played a full season with them.

It was also with the Boston Celtics that Isaiah Thomas finally felt what it was being a winner in the NBA. He would make his first playoff appearance as a member of the Celtics. The seventh-seeded team would go up against a championship favorite Cleveland Cavaliers led by LeBron James in the opening round of the playoffs.

Isaiah Thomas made a remarkable playoff debut in Game 1 of the series. He would go on to penetrate his way against Kyrie Irving, who was drafted 59 spots before him back in 2011. He finished the game with 22 points and ten assists off the bench. In Game 2, he was just as fearless in scoring the ball after going for 22 points. He would, however, struggle in Game 3 scoring only 5 points. Then again, he would attack the rim relentlessly in Game 4 to go for 21 points. Unfortunately for the Celtics, the Cavaliers ended up sweeping them in the series. But it was not a disappoint playoff debut for Isaiah Thomas, who averaged 17.5 points and seven assists against an elite level team.

First All-Star Season

Similar to his first season with the Boston Celtics, Isaiah Thomas started out the 2015-16 season playing behind Marcus Smart at the point guard position. He was the considered the designated sixth man for Brad Stevens, who was looking to build on the success that the young but feisty Boston Celtics saw the previous season. The team still ranked as one of the youngest, if not the youngest, squads in the league. Nevertheless, their lack of experience and age never impeded them from making an impact. Isaiah Thomas would become the frontrunner for the face of the revamped Boston Celtics.

Thomas made his season debut in his first full season with the Boston Celtics on October 28 against the Philadelphia 76ers. Against the struggling franchise, he would put up 27 points on 10 out of 19 shooting off the bench. Thomas played only 29 minutes in that win. He then had 25 points and seven assists off the bench in his next game against the Toronto Raptors. Boston ended up losing that contest before losing another one against the San Antonio Spurs on November 1. IT only had 15 points in that game.

Three games into the young season and Brad Stevens decided to make a change that would benefit not only Isaiah Thomas, but the whole Boston Celtics team. He would start Isaiah Thomas in the fourth game of the season against the Indiana Pacers. The Celtics and their new starting point guard would put up a valiant fight and would only lose by two points. Thomas had 27 points and seven assists in that game while shooting 9 out of 19 from the field and 4 out of 7 from the three-point area.

After starting the season 1-3, the Boston Celtics found themselves winning six of their next eight games ever since Isaiah Thomas was thrust into the starting point guard position. Thomas had his first double-double of the season during that run. He had 23 points, five rebounds, and ten assists in a win over the Atlanta Hawks on November 13. Following that performance, he played well against the bigger and more athletic Russell Westbrook while registering 20 points and eight assists in a win for the Celtics. And a night later on November 16, he had one of the more efficient games of his life in a win against the Houston Rockets. In only 24 minutes, he made 9 of his 12 field goal attempts to score 23 points.

On November 25, Isaiah Thomas topped the 30-point barrier for the first time that season. He finished a win against the Philadelphia 76ers with 30 points scored on 11 out of 21 shooting from the field and 4 out of 7 from the three-point area. Two days later, he was a main catalyst for a 33-point win against the Washington Wizards. He had 21 points in that game. With Isaiah Thomas starting, the Boston Celtics were at a healthy 11-9 throughout their first 20 games of the season.

On December 11, Isaiah Thomas put up a valiant fight against the reigning MVP Stephen Curry in a double-overtime loss to the defending champions Golden State Warriors. Despite struggling from the field, he fed teammates well to record ten assists on top of the 18 points he scored. However, he was unable to stop Curry from dropping 38 points on him during that game. Curry did, however, struggle shooting from the field in that game thanks in large part to how Thomas kept up with him the entire night.

A night after that loss to the Warriors, Isaiah Thomas would go for a season high of 13 assists while also going for 21 points in a matchup against fellow 2011 draftee Kemba Walker, who was chosen more than 50 spots before him. In a battle against two of the best point guards in the 2011 class, Isaiah Thomas outplayed Kemba Walker, who only had 16 points in that game.

On December 16, Isaiah Thomas topped the career high he registered in his third season as a King nearly two years before. He dropped 38 points on 12 out of 20 shooting from the field, 3 out of 5 shooting from the three-point area, and 11 out of 11 from the foul line. He also added seven assists in that loss. Two nights later, he would go for 14 out of 15 from the foul stripe to score 29 points in a loss to the Atlanta Hawks.

It would take a while for Isaiah Thomas to top the 30-point mark for a third time that season. It was on January 10, 2016, when he had 35 big points against the Memphis

Grizzlies. He made 11 of his 19 shots, 4 of his eight three-pointers, and all nine of his free throws in that game while also adding eight assists. Two days later, he would go for 34 points and eight assists against the New York Knicks. Sadly, those two games were the endpoints in what became a four-game losing skid for the Celtics.

Though three of Isaiah Thomas' four 30-point games that season came at losses, he would show that his scoring ways would somehow lead the Celtics to a victory when he led Boston to a win over the Washington Wizards on January 16. Isaiah made only 6 of his 14 field goal attempts that game, but five of those shots were from the three-point territory. He also shot 15 out of 16 from the free-throw line in that match. As January unfolded, Isaiah Thomas was the team's best and most consistent scorer. Nevertheless, the Celtics would win only 8 of their 17 games that month.

Come February, Isaiah Thomas was making a good case as an All-Star reserve when he was playing his consistent scoring self while leading the Boston Celtics to playoff contention. He started the first five games of the month averaging 19.2 points and six assists before going off on

February 10. In that game against no less than Chris Paul, who was considered the best pure point guard in the sport, Thomas tried to match the output of one of history's best playmakers. CP3 finished the game with 35 points and 13 assists. Meanwhile, the competitive fire in Thomas had him going for 36 points and 11 assists while getting the more important win.

Isaiah Thomas' regular performances in leading the Boston Celtics to a chance to make a playoff spot earned him a spot in the 2016 Eastern Conference All-Stars. With that, he became the lowest draft pick to have been named an All-Star. Together with Calvin Murphy, he also became the shortest player to be named an All-Star. Imagine 59 teams passing on him back in 2011 because he was only 5'9". Now the pint-sized scoring point guard had become an All-Star before 55 of his other draftmates. Only Kyrie Irving, Klay Thompson, Kawhi Leonard, and Jimmy Butler became All-Stars out of the 2011 class as of 2016. Kemba Walker would make it a season later, but at that point, only Irving developed into an All-Star among the top 10 draftees of 2011.

During March, it would seem that getting the All-Star nod only made Isaiah Thomas hungrier and more competitive. From March 2 until April 8, Isaiah Thomas put on a scoring barrage, having scored more than 20 points in all of the games he played in that period. Those included back-to-back games of scoring more than 30 points at the beginning of March. He had 30 points on 11 out of 20 shooting from the field in a win against the Portland Trailblazers on March 2 before registering 32 in a win over New York two days later. The other two 30-point games he had was when he put up 30 in a loss to the Rockets on March 11 and then 32 against the New Orleans Pelicans on April 6.

Throughout March of 2016, Isaiah Thomas averaged an impressive 25.9 points and 4.1 assists. He shot nearly 45% from the floor and 42% from the three-point line. And during the 18-game run of scoring more than 20 points per night, he averaged 25.7 points and 4.5 assists while shooting 46.5% from the floor and 42% from deep. More importantly, the Celtics ended up losing only seven of those 18 games. From being the 60th in the 2011 NBA

Draft, Isaiah Thomas was growing into a franchise player for the Boston Celtics.

In his fifth season in the league and his first full one with the Boston Celtics, Isaiah Thomas averaged All-Star numbers of 22.2 points, 6.2 assists, and 1.1 steals. He was once again one of the few players under 6 feet tall to average at least 20 points and at least six assists over an entire season. Isaiah Thomas would also lead the Boston Celtics to a playoff spot for the second season in a row.

Isaiah Thomas and the Boston Celtics would march into the postseason full of confidence against a veteran Atlanta Hawks team. Thomas, in Game 1, would top his playoff career high by scoring 27 points and dishing out eight assists despite. However, his efforts were in vain as the Hawks took Game 1 by merely a point. As the Atlanta Hawks took Game 2 soundly, Thomas was saddled by a 4 of 15 shooting night in that loss.

With his back against the wall and his competitive fire burning ever more brightly, Isaiah Thomas was not willing to cede a 0-3 series lead to the Hawks when the series shifted over to Boston for Games 3 and 4. He played out of his mind in Game 3. Thomas shot 12 out of 24 from the field while running circles around the Hawks' elite defense. He also made 5 of his 12 three-point shots and 13 of his 15 free throws to record an overall career high of 42 points in that win. He joined nine other Celtics players that have scored at least 40 points in a playoff game.

Thomas then led the way in Game 4 with 28 points to help his team tie the series up 2-2. Sadly, he played poorly in what became a blowout loss in Game 5. He was only 3 out of 12 for a total of 7 points in that game. Then, in Game 6, the Hawks completed the series win despite a double-double effort from Thomas, who finished with 25 points and ten assists. IT averaged 24.2 points and five assists in those six tough playoff games.

While the Boston Celtics might have lost in the first round of the playoffs, the biggest positive they could take out of that season was how Isaiah Thomas had grown into a legitimate star in the NBA. At that point of his career, many would already say that Isaiah Thomas had the best season in NBA history for a guy listed at 5'9" and under.

The win shares would say so. Thomas ranks first in league history for any player listed 5'9" or under when it comes to win shares.[v] That was how big an impact he had for such a small package.

At that point of his career, Isaiah Thomas also was no longer playing to prove himself. He had already confirmed that he was wanted in the Celtics locker room. He had already shown that he was a star. There no longer was a chip on his shoulder. He no longer played as if he wanted people to regret not drafting him. He was playing more like himself. His aggression had become controlled and better suited for Brad Stevens' system. He was enjoying the game for the first time since getting drafted.

At the same time, Isaiah Thomas had also grown into a leader for a ridiculously young locker room. He had taken the lessons of Bruce Lee, who he had grown to idolize during the past offseason, to heart. He became more vocal to his teammates while also staying true to their camaraderie. He was not afraid of confronting others, but at the same time, not afraid to pat the heads of his teammates for every play they finished. The relationship between Isaiah Thomas and the Boston Celtics had indeed become one of mutual understanding. The Celtics needed him just as much as he needed to be in Boston.

Rise to Elite Status, the King in the Fourth

What distinguished Isaiah Thomas from all the other players in the league was that he was building on the experience, confidence, and skills he learned from the previous season and took every lesson he got to the next one. He would only get better in the 2016-17 season while his team acquired a key piece in center Al Horford, who was signed from the Atlanta Hawks during the free agency period. While Horford provided the defense and another scoring option for the Celtics, it was Isaiah's growth that ultimately made them a top contender in the Eastern Conference.

As soon as the season began, Isaiah Thomas was in attack mode. He started with 25 points on 7 out of 14 shooting against a struggling Brooklyn Nets team in a win for his Celtics. He also added eight assists and six rebounds in that game. After that, he would finish the next three games scoring at least 23 points. He finished with 23 points and ten assists for his first double-double of the season in a win over the Chicago Bulls on November 2. But that was only the beginning.

Before anyone could notice it, Isaiah Thomas had started piling up the points early on in the season. He had back-to-back games of scoring 30 points in losses to the Cleveland Cavaliers and the Denver Nuggets at the beginning of November. Then, in the middle of the month, he would explode for 37 points on 13 out of 29 shooting from the floor in a one-point loss to the New Orleans Pelicans. He followed that performance up with 30 points two nights later in a win over the Dallas Mavericks.

Early in December, he would again go for a season high of 37 points in a win against the Philadelphia 76ers. He made 11 of his 19 shots from the floor and 13 of his 15 free throws in that game. Two days later on December 5, he scored 20 in a loss to the Houston Rockets. While those 20 points were not impressive, they showed how good of a consistent scorer Thomas is as the pint-sized point guard finished his first 21 games scoring 20 or more points in all but one of those contests. It was also during those first 21 games when Isaiah Thomas mounted a franchise record-shattering personal run.

After missing four games due to a groin strain following that December 5 loss to the Houston Rockets, Isaiah Thomas immediately went back to work. He scored 26 points in his return game in a win over the Charlotte Hornets on December 16. Four days later, he would top his career best in scoring. In an overtime contest against the Memphis Grizzlies, Isaiah Thomas proved his ability to come up big in the clutch by scoring 36 points in the second half alone. He made 10 of his 16 field goal attempts, 7 of his ten three-pointers, and all 17 of his free throws to record a new career best of 44 points. Performances like that and the ones that followed after it earned him Player of the Week honors.

The developing story about Isaiah Thomas at that point of the season was how clutch and how big of a performer he had become in the fourth quarter. No game showed his fourth quarter proficiency more than what would become a new career outing for him in the Celtics' final contest for the year 2016. In that game against the Miami Heat, Isaiah

Thomas entered the fourth quarter with 23 points. He ended the game with a career high of 52 points. Thomas had scored 29 alone in the fourth quarter. He made 15 of his 26 shots, a career best 9 out of 13 from the three-point line, and all 13 of his free throws in that game. His 52 points rank fourth in Celtics history. More importantly, he was quickly becoming known as "The King in the Fourth," a nickname made in reference to *Game of Thrones'* "King of the North."

Isaiah Thomas did not slow down one bit. In his first game for the year 2017, he finished with 29 points on 10 out of 18 shooting from the field in a win over the Utah Jazz. More importantly, he dished out a career-high 15 assists in a two-game span that saw him breaking his career records in both points and dimes. He then finished the next eight games scoring 30 or more points in five of those outings.

One of the five games in that run was one wherein he scored 41 points on 14 out of 28 shooting in a loss to the Portland Trailblazers. Before that match, he had 39 in a loss to the New York Knicks. And before that loss to the Knicks, he had 35 in a win against Charlotte. But those performances were not even the best he would put up that month.

Following that 41-point game in a loss to the Portland Trailblazers, Isaiah Thomas would go on to score 38 on the Houston Rockets on January 25 in a win. Three days later, he would drop 37 points on 11 out of 21 shooting from the field against the Milwaukee Bucks. Ending the month of January on a high note, he finished with 41 points in a victory over the Detroit Pistons. He led the league in scoring for the month of January after having averaged nearly 33 points. He had also slowly crept up to become the second leading scorer in the league behind only Russell Westbrook in that department. Because of that, he was named Eastern Conference Player of the Month.

He would not take things easier during the month of February. Isaiah Thomas started the month by scoring 44 points on 12 out of 22 shooting from the field, 5 out of 12 from the three-point line, and 15 out of 16 from the free-throw line in a win against the Toronto Raptors. Two days later on February 3 in a rivalry game against the Lakers, he finished with 38 big points in a win. And a few days before the All-Star break, he would go for 33 points in a win against the Philadelphia 76ers as he was on his way to his second consecutive appearance in the midseason classic. That performance against the 76ers tied the record set by legendary Celtic John Havlicek for most consecutive games scoring 20 or more points. It was number 40.

On February 16 right before he was on his way to New Orleans for the All-Star Game, Isaiah Thomas would earn the record for most consecutive games of scoring 20 or more points. He had 29 points in a loss to the Chicago Bulls that night. Who would have ever thought that a 5'9" point guard picked dead last in the 2011 NBA Draft would someday score 20 or more points in 41 consecutive games for the most storied franchise in the NBA?

Shortly after the All-Star break on February 27, the record was cut short after Thomas only scored 19 points in a loss to the Atlanta Hawks. The record ended at 43 games, but it would seem unlikely for anyone to break it anytime soon. Even after the record was snapped, Thomas would only score less than 20 points in one of the next nine games he played. Throughout the season, he would only score less than 20 points thrice.

Isaiah Thomas is currently averaging 29.2 points and six assists. He ranks third behind Russell Westbrook and James Harden concerning scoring but is arguably just as good considering he is only 5'9". More impressively, nobody thought that a man of his height would be shooting career bests of 46.2% from the floor and 38.3% from the three-point line that season. Isaiah Thomas can no longer call himself a mere star. He had become an elite player in a league dominated by point guards. He ranks among the top guys in that category. More importantly, the Celtics currently stand 46-26 only behind the Cleveland Cavaliers in the standings. From overlooked player, to All-Star, to elite point guard, and now to MVP contender.

Chapter 5: Personal Life

Isaiah Thomas' parents are James "Keith" Thomas and Tina Baldtrip. His name comes from the Detroit Pistons legend Isiah Thomas after his father lost a bet to his best friend. James bet that the Los Angeles Lakers would beat the Detroit Pistons in the NBA Finals back in the late 80's, but Detroit ended up sweeping the series. Thus, James would then name his son after the point guard that dominated his Lakers. However, Tina would change the spelling of the name to make it more religious so that it would fit her family's Pentecostal background. She named her son "Isaiah," which was spelled the same as the biblical name.

Isaiah Thomas is married to Kayla Wallace. The ceremony happened in 2016 in Seattle, where Thomas grew up. He already had two sons with his longtime girlfriend, now wife. The first son is James, who is about six years old. He lives with Thomas' mother in Seattle. The second one is Jaiden, who lives with the couple in Boston.

Isaiah Thomas also keeps a group of Seattle-based NBA player within his close circle. Since he was a young boy playing in Washington, he has always been close with NBA legends such as Jason Terry and Jamal Crawford. Both those older players have served as inspirations and mentors to the young Isaiah Thomas. Speaking of mentors, Isaiah has also developed a relationship with the older Isiah, who has kept in touch with his NBA journey. The older Thomas was one of the first people to congratulate him when he was traded to the Boston Celtics.

Chapter 6: Impact on Basketball

When you talk about impact, how much of an impact could a 5'9" point guard have in a league that puts a lot of premium on size? Would a pint-sized player even have an influence in the NBA, which is dominated by some of the biggest and strongest athletes to walk the face of the earth? Despite Isaiah Thomas' meager size, nobody could ever discount the impact he has had on the game of basketball.

The league was never short of players listed under 6 feet tall. The likes of Calvin Murphy, Muggsy Bogues, Earl Boykins, and Damon Stoudamire have all made it to NBA despite their lack of size. However, those players have all been called up to the league not because they could score points, but because they knew how to play the point guard position the right way—by making plays for others.

Save for Calvin Murphy, who played in an NBA era where players were not as big and athletic as they are now, all the other short NBA players that were able to make an impact in the league were known for their capability to make plays. Bogues, Boykins, and Stoudamire, among others, were best known for their ability to make plays and run offenses fluidly. When it came down to passing and making plays, the disadvantage of being small was minimized. But here comes Isaiah Thomas.

Ever since he was a young boy, Thomas had always been a scoring guard. He learned how to score over bigger defenders by watching the NBA's best scoring point guards. If not that, he took what the defense gave him and learned by experience how to score inside the paint despite being a lot smaller than the trees guarding the basket. He also developed a nice shooting touch out on the perimeter ad beyond the three-point line in case his ability to get to the basket was taken away. This was a pint-sized guard who was born and bred to be a scorer.

However, nobody believed he could score at the NBA level. Nobody thought he could translate into a passing point guard in the NBA. Nobody thought he could defend the bigger and more athletic players in the professional league. Simply put, nobody believed in what Isaiah Thomas could do if ever he does make it to the NBA.

As gifted a scorer as Isaiah Thomas is, that kind of a mentality was what nearly got him undrafted. He was picked dead last in the 2011 NBA Draft mainly because nobody believed he could take his scoring skills to the professional level given his lack of size. He was passed up 59 times. Had they not been desperate for a point guard, the Sacramento Kings might not have even drafted him with the 60th of that year's draft.

That was the theme of Isaiah Thomas' early career in basketball. He was overlooked. It did not matter how much points he scored in high school. It did not matter that he averaged over 16 points during his college career. What mattered was his size. What mattered was that his playing style did not fit the body he was gifted with. However, what mattered most for Isaiah Thomas was how much he believed in himself. He knew that he was a star, and he never gave up on that belief.

As soon as Isaiah Thomas got a chance to prove himself, he took it. He played with a huge chip on his shoulder in his rookie season with the Sacramento Kings. He never changed the way he played. He was always aggressive. He attacked the paint, made shots he knew he could make, broke defenses out on the perimeter, and made the right passes when he needed to. Thomas continued to play the way he always did. That was what brought him to the dance.

However, despite proving himself worthy of a spot in the NBA by scoring at will even for his size, he was overlooked yet again. The Sacramento Kings had no need for a point guard that looked to score more than to pass the ball. They loved how Isaiah Thomas broke defenses down, but they wanted him to dish the ball to DeMarcus Cousins and Rudy Gay among others. They wanted him to be able to defend opposing point guards at a time when the league was dominated by some of the beset playmakers in NBA history. Simply put, they undervalued what Thomas brought to the floor.

But while the Phoenix Suns loved how aggressive a scorer Isaiah Thomas always was, it was a marriage bound to fail. They valued two other point guards more than they did Thomas. There were chemistry issues in the team mainly because the staff wanted to play three scoring point guards at the same time. It was a partnership that lasted only 46 games.

The failure with the Phoenix Suns was what ultimately landed Isaiah Thomas with the right team. The Boston Celtics have long wanted a player of his aggressive nature without even considering how small he was. They needed a leader and a scorer that could start offenses for a team of inexperienced youngsters in the early parts of their 20's. That was what Isaiah Thomas brought to the Celtics.

It would not take too long for Thomas to bloom into an All-Star leader for the Boston Celtics. He took the coaching staff and his teammate's trust with him and played naturally, similar to how he did when he was in high school and college. The team went along with him. He broke defenses down with his quickness and craftiness. His teammates waited in their spots in case he dished the ball out to them. If not, they were happy enough to see the ball going down the hoop from all the shifty plays Isaiah Thomas had to make. Soon enough, Thomas would average nearly 30 points for a Boston Celtics team that believed in what he could do.

Now, when you ask what kind of an impact Thomas has had on basketball, one would say that he made himself matter despite his size. Isaiah Thomas put his heart and soul in every play, no matter how big his defender and the shot blocker were. He never stopped believing in his skills and his abilities. He never let criticism and lack of belief get in the way of his confidence. He never changed the way he played, and that was what made him one of the elite scorers the NBA has to offer today.

Five years ago, one would laugh at disbelief that a 5'9" scoring point guard is averaging nearly 30 points a night and is one of the leading contenders for the MVP award. Today, Thomas would put to shame such laughter. He showed that the NBA is not a league where size mattered. What mattered most was how much you believe in yourself despite all odds stacking up against you. That was the impact Thomas had on the game of basketball.

Isaiah Thomas, in his short six-year NBA career, has shown that short players can still indeed become great scorers in the league. He showed his leadership quality as the main gun and the new face of the Boston Celtics. He showed how great of a player he is by leading his team not only in scoring and assists but also regarding leadership and attitude. He brought his hardworking mantra to a blue collar team. He made the Boston Celtics relevant again when other teams thought he would not even make the NBA back in 2011. Thomas defied odds and made the biggest impact that a compact 5'9" player could make.

Chapter 7: Legacy and Future

Calvin Murphy, Isiah Thomas, and Allen Iverson were some of league history's best scorers at 6 feet tall or under. Size never mattered to those guys whenever they decided they wanted to put the ball into the hoop. Height never mattered to them whenever they wanted to win games and make an impact not only to their team, but the whole NBA landscape as well. Heart mattered more to them than their lack of size. This is a legacy that Isaiah Thomas continues today.

Isaiah Thomas was often overlooked particularly because he was a scoring point guard that lacked a lot of size. But he never let criticism and lack of belief get in the way of his quest for greatness. He stuck to the way he played and made himself matter in a league that puts a lot of premium on size. Isaiah Thomas continues the legacy that little guys before him started. He made skill and heart matter more than size ever did.

Isaiah Thomas' journey to the NBA is also a legacy of its own. He was nearly undrafted back in 2011. He was drafted as the final pick of the 2011 NBA Draft only because the Sacramento Kings needed a point guard on their roster. Despite the organizations' lack of confidence in what he brought, Thomas worked harder and harder while never changing his approach to the game. He never changed his style, even when the Kings gave him away because he was not a good passer. He never changed his style even while he was playing together with two other scoring point guards in Phoenix. And he never changed his style, particularly because that was what the Boston Celtics loved about him.

Isaiah Thomas always knew he was going to be a star someday in the NBA. He knew it the moment he first shot a basketball through a hoop when he was a youngster. He knew it the very moment his name was called as the final pick of the 2011 NBA Draft. All he needed was the right team to believe in the same things he did. That was where the Boston Celtics came in.

The Celtics and Isaiah Thomas were a perfect marriage. The organization loved the way he played because that was precisely why they traded for him in the first place. And the city of Boston loved their new star. The Boston Celtics have always been one of the most storied franchises in the history of the league. Jerseys that belong to guys such as Bill Russell, Sam Jones, Bob Cousy, John Havlicek, and Larry Bird, among others, hang in the rafters of the TD Garden in Boston. Those legends have all earned the adoration of the Boston crowd because of how they put their heart on the line every single game. Isaiah Thomas was never different from that.

Every single night, Thomas played as if he was just as big as, or even bigger than, his defenders. He never cared how much height he lacked or how big his opponents were. All he cared about was the size of his heart. This earned him the adoration of the crowd. This earned him the reputation as the new face of one of history's most successful sports franchises.

Isaiah Thomas never took the trust and confidence given to him by the coaching staff and the people of Boston for granted. In fact, it was what fueled him to become better. He would become one of the best scorers in the entire NBA despite his lack of size to physically contend with the likes of Russell Westbrook, Kevin Durant, and James Harden. He would even become the best scorer in the quarter that mattered most. Dubbed as the King in the Fourth, Isaiah Thomas had also become the best closer in the league because of how much points he scores during the fourth quarter. Nobody would ever expect that from a man standing 5'9".

Given how many points he is scoring and how well he is leading the Boston Celtics in today's NBA, one would argue that Isaiah Thomas had become the best player listed under 6 feet tall in league history. No other player of his size or smaller had scored the same amount of points or made the same impact as he did to a winning team. You would even rarely see players over 6 feet tall scoring 29 points a night, but Isaiah Thomas does it in the smallest package possible.

Though he may still be far from being called the best little man in league history, there is no doubting that Isaiah Thomas is having the best season the NBA has ever seen from a man standing 5'9" or under. Not even Calvin Murphy nor Muggsy Bogues have ever had the same season that Thomas is having. He does not even do it by being a volume shooter. He is shooting well above 46% from the floor. That was something not even Allen Iverson could do during his best seasons. That speaks a lot to how efficient, consistent, and celebrated a scorer Isaiah Thomas had developed into.

At 22.2 points per game throughout his career, Isaiah Thomas is the NBA's best scoring player standing 5'9" or under. He still has a chance to up that average in the following seasons considering he still in the prime of his career. At 27 years old, Thomas has several years left until he finally hangs up his boots. He is still in his sixth year of his NBA seasons and could have as much as ten more seasons more if he keeps himself healthy and in shape.

And if indeed this season is not a fluke and if indeed Isaiah Thomas keeps himself in shape for the following seasons, it may not be a far off conclusion that he would someday be called the best little man in league history. A championship for a surging Boston Celtics team might cement that legacy. But as of now, he is doing fine in earning that title just by being himself on a team that accepts everything he does on the floor.

Isaiah Thomas has defied gravity and odds to get to where he is. Now all he has left to do is to challenge his limits to get to the pinnacle of NBA greatness. And when he gets to that pinnacle, one would always remember that he is only 5'9" standing among greats that are nearly a foot taller than he is.

Final Word/About the Author

I was born and raised in Norwalk, Connecticut. Growing up, I could often be found spending many nights watching basketball, soccer, and football matches with my father in the family living room. I love sports and everything that sports can embody. I believe that sports are one of most genuine forms of competition, heart, and determination. I write my works to learn more about influential athletes in the hopes that from my writing, you the reader can walk away inspired to put in an equal if not greater amount of hard work and perseverance to pursue your goals. If you enjoyed *Isaiah Thomas: The Inspiring Story of One of Basketball's Most Prolific Point Guards,* please leave a review! Also, you can read more of my works on *Roger Federer, Novak Djokovic, Andrew Luck, Rob Gronkowski, Brett Favre, Calvin Johnson, Drew Brees, J.J. Watt, Colin Kaepernick, Aaron Rodgers, Peyton Manning, Tom Brady, Russell Wilson, Michael Jordan, LeBron James, Kyrie Irving, Klay Thompson, Stephen Curry, Kevin Durant, Russell Westbrook, Anthony Davis, Chris Paul, Blake Griffin, Kobe Bryant, Joakim Noah, Scottie Pippen,*

Carmelo Anthony, Kevin Love, Grant Hill, Tracy McGrady, Vince Carter, Patrick Ewing, Karl Malone, Tony Parker, Allen Iverson, Hakeem Olajuwon, Reggie Miller, Michael Carter-Williams, John Wall, James Harden, Tim Duncan, Steve Nash, Draymond Green, Kawhi Leonard, Dwyane Wade, Ray Allen, Pau Gasol, Dirk Nowitzki, Jimmy Butler, Paul Pierce, Manu Ginobili, Pete Maravich, Larry Bird, Kyle Lowry, Jason Kidd, David Robinson, LaMarcus Aldridge, Derrick Rose, Paul George, Kevin Garnett, Chris Paul, Marc Gasol, Yao Ming, Al Horford and Amar'e Stoudemire in the Kindle Store. If you love basketball, check out my website at claytongeoffreys.com to join my exclusive list where I let you know about my latest books and give you lots of goodies.

Like what you read? Please leave a review!

I write because I love sharing the stories of influential people like Isaiah Thomas with fantastic readers like you. My readers inspire me to write more so please do not hesitate to let me know what you thought by leaving a review! If you love books on life, basketball, or productivity, check out my website at claytongeoffreys.com to join my exclusive list where I let you know about my latest books. Aside from being the first to hear about my latest releases, you can also download a free copy of *33 Life Lessons: Success Principles, Career Advice & Habits of Successful People*. See you there!

Clayton

References

[i] Watanabe, Ben. "Isaiah Thomas' Name Comes From Lakers-Fan Dad Making Ill-Advised Bet". *NESN*. 20 February 2015. Web

[ii] Layden, Tim. "The Little Ticket". *Sports Illustrated*. 8 February 2017. Web

[iii] Jackson, Ryan. "The Rise of Isaiah Thomas". *Fox Sports*. 16 January 2017. Web

[iv] Jones, Jason. "Rejected as a King, Isaiah Thomas Returns to Sacramento Hailed as a Celtic". *The Sacramento Bee*. Web

[v] Flannery, Paul. "All Isaiah Thomas Needed was to be Wanted". *SB Nation*. 5 April 2016

Made in the USA
Columbia, SC
15 September 2017